Mastering Life's Chall

Self-Developm

Julia Popova

Copyright © [2023]

Title: Mastering Life's Challenges: A Guide to
Self-Development for All

Author's: Julia Popova.

This book was printed and published by [Publisher's: Julia Popova] in [2023]

ISBN:

TABLE OF CONTENTS

Chapter 10: Sustaining Self-Development

Conclusion: The Journey of Self-Development

Chapter 1: Understanding Self-Development

The Importance of Self-Development

In our fast-paced and ever-changing world, self-development has become increasingly vital for individuals from all walks of life. Whether you are a student, a professional, a parent, or a retiree, the pursuit of self-development can significantly impact various aspects of your life. This subchapter aims to shed light on the importance of self-development and how it can positively influence your personal growth and success.

Self-development refers to the conscious and continuous effort to improve oneself mentally, emotionally, physically, and spiritually. It is an ongoing process that involves setting goals, acquiring new skills, expanding knowledge, and cultivating positive habits. By dedicating time and energy to self-development, you can enhance your self-awareness, boost your confidence, and unlock your full potential.

One of the key benefits of self-development is personal growth. By engaging in continuous learning and self-reflection, you can identify your strengths and weaknesses, enabling you to make informed decisions and take actions that align with your values and aspirations. Self-development empowers you to embrace change, adapt to new circumstances, and overcome challenges with resilience and determination.

Furthermore, self-development plays a crucial role in professional success. In today's competitive job market, employers seek individuals who are adaptable, proactive, and willing to learn. By investing in self-development, you can stay ahead in your career by acquiring new skills, expanding your knowledge base, and developing a growth mindset. This not only improves your employability but also opens doors to new opportunities and advancement.

Self-development also positively impacts your relationships and overall well-being. By working on yourself, you become more self-aware, emotionally intelligent, and empathetic. This enables you to foster healthier and more meaningful connections with others. Moreover, self-development allows you to prioritize self-care, manage stress, and maintain a positive mindset, leading to improved mental and physical health.

Regardless of your age or background, self-development is a lifelong journey that offers endless possibilities for personal growth and fulfillment. It is a commitment to becoming the best version of yourself and creating a life that aligns with your values and goals. So, embrace the importance of self-development and embark on this transformative journey to unlock your true potential and master life's challenges.

Defining Self-Development

In today's fast-paced and ever-changing world, the concept of self-development has gained significant attention and relevance. But what exactly does self-development mean? How can it benefit us in our personal and professional lives? In this subchapter, we will delve into the essence of self-development and explore its importance for everyone seeking personal growth and success.

Self-development, at its core, is the conscious and continuous pursuit of personal growth, improvement, and self-awareness. It involves taking deliberate actions to enhance various aspects of our lives, including our physical, mental, emotional, and spiritual well-being. Self-development is not a destination but rather a lifelong journey, as we continually strive to become the best versions of ourselves.

One of the key aspects of self-development is self-awareness. It is the ability to understand our strengths, weaknesses, values, beliefs, and emotions. By developing self-awareness, we gain a deeper understanding of ourselves, our motivations, and our behaviors. This knowledge empowers us to make conscious choices and take actions that align with our true desires and aspirations.

Self-development is not limited to a specific niche or audience; it is relevant to everyone. Whether you are a student, professional, parent, or retiree, self-development can bring immense value to your life. It equips us with the necessary tools to navigate life's challenges, make informed decisions, and achieve our goals.

Engaging in self-development activities can lead to numerous benefits. It enhances our personal growth, boosts our confidence, and improves our overall well-being. By continuously learning and growing, we become more adaptable, resilient, and open-minded individuals. Self-development also fosters a sense of purpose and fulfillment, as we strive to live a life that aligns with our values and passions.

There are various ways to embark on the journey of self-development. It could involve reading books, attending workshops or seminars, seeking guidance from mentors or coaches, practicing mindfulness and meditation, or engaging in physical activities. The key is to find what resonates with you and commit to a lifelong process of learning and growth.

In conclusion, self-development is a vital aspect of our lives, regardless of our age, background, or profession. It enables us to unlock our full potential, discover our true selves, and lead more fulfilling lives. By embracing self-development, we embark on a transformative journey of personal growth and empowerment, paving the way for a brighter and more successful future.

Benefits of Self-Development

In today's fast-paced and competitive world, self-development has become more important than ever before. Whether you are a working professional, a student, or an entrepreneur, investing in your personal growth and development can have a profound impact on every aspect of your life. This subchapter in "Mastering Life's Challenges: A Guide to Self-Development for All" focuses on the numerous benefits that self-development can bring to individuals from all walks of life.

One of the key benefits of self-development is increased self-awareness. Through self-reflection, introspection, and self-assessment exercises, you gain a deeper understanding of your strengths, weaknesses, values, and aspirations. This self-awareness allows you to make more informed decisions, align your actions with your goals, and ultimately lead a more fulfilling life.

Self-development also leads to personal growth and improvement. By actively seeking new knowledge and skills, you expand your capabilities, enhance your problem-solving abilities, and become more adaptable to change. Continuous learning and development enable you to stay ahead in your career, increase your earning potential, and open doors to new opportunities.

Furthermore, self-development contributes to improved mental and emotional well-being. Engaging in activities such as mindfulness, meditation, and positive thinking helps you manage stress, reduce anxiety, and cultivate a positive mindset. It empowers you to take control of your emotions, build resilience, and maintain a healthy work-life balance.

Another significant benefit of self-development is enhanced relationships. As you work on yourself, you become more empathetic, compassionate, and understanding towards others. Your improved communication skills and emotional intelligence enable you to build stronger connections, resolve conflicts, and foster healthier relationships both personally and professionally.

Self-development also plays a vital role in boosting self-confidence and self-esteem. As you achieve personal growth milestones and overcome challenges, you develop a sense of pride and belief in your abilities. This newfound confidence allows you to take on bigger challenges, step out of your comfort zone, and seize opportunities that you once thought were beyond your reach.

Ultimately, self-development is a lifelong journey that empowers you to become the best version of yourself. By investing in your personal growth, you not only improve your own life, but you also become a source of inspiration for others. So, regardless of your age, background, or circumstances, embrace the benefits of self-development and unlock your full potential.

Common Misconceptions about Self-Development

Self-development is a journey that everyone should embark on to achieve personal growth, fulfillment, and overall well-being. It is a process of continuous learning, self-reflection, and improvement that helps individuals reach their full potential. However, there are several common misconceptions about self-development that often prevent people from fully embracing this transformative path. In this subchapter, we will debunk these misconceptions and shed light on the true essence of self-development.

One common misconception is that self-development is only for those who are struggling or facing major challenges in life. This couldn't be further from the truth. Self-development is for everyone, regardless of their current situation or level of success. It is about constantly striving to become a better version of oneself and continuously learning and growing, regardless of where one is in life.

Another misconception is that self-development is a selfish endeavor. Some individuals believe that focusing on personal growth and improvement means neglecting their responsibilities towards others. However, self-development is actually a selfless act that benefits not only the individual but also those around them. By becoming the best version of ourselves, we can positively impact our relationships, work, and community, inspiring others to do the same.

It is also often believed that self-development requires a significant amount of time and resources. While dedicating time to self-reflection and growth is crucial, it doesn't necessarily mean hours spent in solitude or expensive workshops. Self-development can be integrated into our daily lives through small, consistent actions such as reading books, listening to podcasts, practicing mindfulness, or seeking feedback from others. It is a gradual process that can be customized to fit our unique lifestyles and circumstances.

Furthermore, there is a misconception that self-development is a linear journey with a clear endpoint. In reality, self-development is an ongoing process that has no definitive destination. It is about embracing change, adapting to new circumstances, and continuously setting new goals for personal growth. Each individual's journey is unique, and there is no one-size-fits-all approach to self-development.

In conclusion, self-development is not limited to a select few or a specific stage of life. It is a transformative path that benefits everyone, regardless of their current situation. It is a selfless act that positively impacts not only the individual but also their relationships, work, and community. Self-development is a gradual process that can be integrated into daily life through small, consistent actions. It is an ongoing journey with no fixed endpoint, allowing individuals to continuously learn, grow, and reach their full potential. By debunking these common misconceptions, we hope to inspire every individual to embrace self-development and embark on a path of personal growth and fulfillment.

Chapter 2: Identifying Personal Challenges

Self-Reflection and Awareness

In the journey of self-development, one of the most powerful tools at our disposal is self-reflection and awareness. It is the cornerstone of personal growth, allowing us to understand ourselves better and make positive changes in our lives. This subchapter will explore the significance of self-reflection and provide practical strategies to cultivate self-awareness.

Self-reflection is the process of introspection, where we pause and examine our thoughts, emotions, and actions. It requires taking a step back from the hustle and bustle of everyday life to gain a deeper understanding of who we are and what drives us. By engaging in self-reflection, we can identify our strengths, weaknesses, and areas for improvement.

Awareness, on the other hand, is the ability to perceive and understand our thoughts, feelings, and behaviors in real-time. It involves being present in the moment and observing ourselves without judgment. Developing self-awareness enables us to recognize patterns, triggers, and habits that may be holding us back from reaching our full potential.

Why is self-reflection and awareness crucial for self-development? Firstly, they allow us to take responsibility for our actions and choices. By understanding our motivations and thought processes, we can make conscious decisions aligned with our values and goals. This empowers us to create the life we truly desire.

Secondly, self-reflection and awareness promote personal growth. When we delve deep into ourselves, we uncover hidden beliefs, fears, and limiting beliefs that may be hindering our progress. By shining a light on these aspects, we can challenge and transform them, unlocking our true potential.

To cultivate self-reflection and awareness, it is essential to create dedicated time for introspection. This may involve journaling, meditation, or simply finding a quiet space to think. Regularly ask yourself thought-provoking questions such as "What are my core values?", "What are my strengths and weaknesses?", and "What is my vision for the future?".

Additionally, seek feedback from trusted friends, mentors, or coaches who can provide an outside perspective. Their insights can help us identify blind spots and gain a more accurate understanding of ourselves.

Remember, self-reflection and awareness are ongoing practices that require patience and commitment. As we continue to delve deeper into ourselves, we unlock new layers of understanding and growth. Embrace this journey, for it is through self-reflection and awareness that we can truly master life's challenges and become the best versions of ourselves.

In conclusion, self-reflection and awareness are vital components of self-development. They empower us to gain a deeper understanding of ourselves, make conscious choices, and overcome obstacles. By cultivating self-reflection and awareness, we embark on a transformative journey of personal growth and fulfillment.

Recognizing Limiting Beliefs

In our journey of self-development, one crucial aspect that often goes unnoticed is the recognition of limiting beliefs. These beliefs act as invisible barriers, holding us back from reaching our true potential and living a fulfilling life. To truly master life's challenges, we must first identify and challenge these limiting beliefs.

Limiting beliefs are deeply ingrained thoughts or assumptions we hold about ourselves, others, and the world around us. They are often formed during our childhood or through past experiences, shaping our perception of what is possible and what is not. These beliefs can manifest in various areas of our lives, be it relationships, career, health, or personal growth.

The first step towards recognizing limiting beliefs is self-awareness. We must cultivate the ability to observe our thoughts and patterns objectively. Take a moment to reflect on your inner dialogue and pay attention to recurring themes or negative self-talk. Are there any thoughts that consistently hold you back or make you doubt your abilities? These are likely your limiting beliefs.

Once identified, it is essential to question the validity of these beliefs. Ask yourself, "Is this belief based on factual evidence or just a perception?" Often, we realize that these beliefs are based on past experiences or fear rather than actual truth. By challenging these beliefs, we open up possibilities for growth and transformation.

Another effective technique to recognize limiting beliefs is to examine the stories we tell ourselves. We all have personal narratives that shape our identity and influence our actions. These stories can either empower us or reinforce our limitations. By becoming aware of the stories we tell ourselves, we can identify the beliefs that no longer serve us and rewrite a new narrative that aligns with our aspirations.

Recognizing limiting beliefs is a continuous process that requires patience and self-reflection. It may involve seeking support from mentors, therapists, or joining self-development communities. Surrounding ourselves with like-minded individuals who are also on a journey of self-discovery can provide valuable insights and encouragement.

In conclusion, recognizing limiting beliefs is a vital step in self-development. By identifying these beliefs, questioning their validity, and rewriting our narratives, we can break free from the barriers that hold us back. Remember, you have the power to shape your reality and overcome any limiting belief that stands in your way. Embrace the journey of self-discovery, and unlock your true potential.

Identifying Negative Patterns

In our journey of self-development, it is crucial to recognize and understand the negative patterns that hinder our progress. These patterns can manifest in various aspects of our lives, affecting our relationships, career, and overall well-being. By identifying these patterns, we empower ourselves to break free from their grip and create a more fulfilling life.

Negative patterns can be subtle and elusive, making it challenging to pinpoint their origin. However, with self-awareness and a willingness to delve deeper, we can unravel these patterns and gain control over them.

One common negative pattern is self-sabotage, where we unknowingly undermine our own success and happiness. It often stems from limiting beliefs, such as feeling unworthy or fearing failure. By recognizing these beliefs and challenging their validity, we can replace them with positive affirmations and build a healthier mindset.

Another negative pattern is repeating toxic relationships or attracting similar circumstances repeatedly. This pattern may arise from unresolved emotional wounds or a lack of self-worth. By reflecting on past relationships and experiences, we can identify commonalities and gain insight into the root cause. With this awareness, we can work on healing ourselves and setting healthier boundaries.

Procrastination is yet another negative pattern that many struggle with. It often arises from fear, perfectionism, or a lack of clarity. By identifying the underlying reasons for procrastination, we can develop strategies to overcome it. Breaking tasks into smaller, manageable steps, setting deadlines, and seeking support can help us tackle procrastination head-on.

Identifying negative patterns requires self-reflection and a willingness to confront uncomfortable truths. It may be helpful to keep a journal, where we can document our thoughts, emotions, and recurring themes in our lives. Seeking guidance from a therapist or a trusted mentor can also provide valuable insights and support during this process.

Remember, self-development is a lifelong journey, and identifying negative patterns is just the first step. Once we become aware of these patterns, we can actively work on replacing them with positive habits and beliefs. By doing so, we empower ourselves to live a life filled with growth, resilience, and self-fulfillment.

In conclusion, recognizing and understanding negative patterns is essential for self-development. By identifying patterns such as self-sabotage, toxic relationships, and procrastination, we can take the necessary steps to break free from their hold. Through self-reflection, seeking support, and implementing positive changes, we can transform our lives and create a brighter future. Remember, you have the power to master life's challenges and become the best version of yourself.

Overcoming Fear and Resistance

Fear and resistance are two powerful emotions that can hold us back from reaching our full potential. They often manifest as obstacles on our journey of self-development. However, with the right mindset and strategies, we can learn to conquer these fears and break through the resistance that stands in our way.

One of the first steps in overcoming fear is to recognize and acknowledge it. Fear can take various forms, such as fear of failure, fear of judgment, or fear of the unknown. By identifying these fears, we can begin to understand their origins and the impact they have on our lives. This self-awareness is crucial in order to move forward and make positive changes.

Once we have identified our fears, it is important to confront them head-on. This may involve stepping outside of our comfort zones and taking risks. It is natural to feel apprehensive, but by gradually exposing ourselves to the things that scare us, we can gradually build up our confidence and diminish the power of fear.

Another effective strategy for overcoming fear and resistance is to reframe our thoughts. Often, our fears are rooted in negative beliefs or assumptions. By challenging these thoughts and replacing them with more positive and empowering ones, we can change our perspective and approach challenges with a renewed sense of confidence.

Furthermore, seeking support from others can be incredibly beneficial on our journey of self-development. Surrounding ourselves with a network of like-minded individuals who understand our struggles and can offer guidance and encouragement can make a significant difference. Whether it is through joining a support group, seeking a mentor, or simply sharing our experiences with trusted friends, the power of community cannot be underestimated.

Additionally, practicing self-care is vital in overcoming fear and resistance. Engaging in activities that bring us joy and relaxation can help reduce stress and anxiety, enabling us to face our fears with a clearer mind. This may include exercising, meditating, spending time in nature, or engaging in creative pursuits.

In conclusion, fear and resistance are common obstacles on our path of self-development. However, by recognizing and acknowledging our fears, confronting them head-on, reframing our thoughts, seeking support, and practicing self-care, we can overcome these barriers and continue to grow and evolve. Remember, the journey of self-development is a lifelong process, and it is through facing our fears that we discover our true potential.

Chapter 3: Setting Personal Goals

The Power of Goal Setting

Setting goals is a fundamental aspect of personal development and achieving success in every area of life. Whether you are a student, professional, entrepreneur, or a homemaker, setting goals can significantly impact your journey towards self-improvement. In this subchapter, we will explore the power of goal setting and how it can transform your life.

Goals provide direction and purpose. Without clear goals, we often find ourselves drifting aimlessly, unsure of what we truly want to achieve. By setting specific, measurable, achievable, relevant, and time-bound (SMART) goals, we give ourselves a target to strive for. Goals act as a roadmap, guiding us towards our desired destination and ensuring we stay on track.

Goal setting fosters motivation and inspiration. When we set goals, we create a vision of what we want to accomplish, igniting a fire within us. Goals help us channel our energy towards meaningful actions, driving us to push beyond our limits and overcome obstacles. The progress we make towards our goals fuels our motivation, providing a sense of accomplishment and propelling us forward.

Goals enhance focus and concentration. With a multitude of distractions in today's fast-paced world, it is easy to lose sight of our priorities. By setting goals, we prioritize our aspirations and filter out distractions that hinder our progress. Goals enable us to concentrate on the tasks that truly matter, enabling us to be more productive and efficient in our endeavors.

Goal setting promotes personal growth. As we strive to achieve our goals, we inevitably face challenges and setbacks. These obstacles provide valuable opportunities for learning, self-reflection, and growth. By overcoming these hurdles, we develop resilience, determination, and a deeper understanding of ourselves. Each goal achieved becomes a stepping stone towards personal growth and self-actualization.

Goal setting breeds success. By setting clear goals and working towards them consistently, we increase our chances of success. Goals provide us with a sense of purpose, direction, and focus, allowing us to make better decisions and take calculated risks. As we achieve our goals, we build confidence in our abilities and create a positive feedback loop of success, propelling us towards even greater achievements.

In conclusion, goal setting is a powerful tool that can transform your life. By setting goals, you unleash your potential, increase your motivation, enhance your focus, foster personal growth, and breed success. Whether you are embarking on a new career, improving your health and well-being, or seeking personal fulfillment, harness the power of goal setting to master life's challenges and embark on a journey of self-development. Start now, and witness the incredible transformation that goal setting can bring to every aspect of your life.

Creating SMART Goals

Setting goals is an essential part of personal growth and self-development. Without clear objectives, we may find ourselves drifting through life without a sense of purpose or direction. However, simply setting goals is not enough; it is equally important to make sure they are SMART goals – specific, measurable, achievable, relevant, and time-bound. In this chapter, we will explore the process of creating SMART goals and how they can greatly enhance our self-development journey.

Specific goals are clear and well-defined. They answer the questions of what, why, and how. By having a specific goal, we are better able to focus our energy and resources towards achieving it. Measurable goals are quantifiable and allow us to track our progress. They provide a sense of accomplishment and motivation as we see ourselves moving closer to our desired outcome.

Achievable goals are realistic and within reach. While it is important to challenge ourselves, setting unattainable goals can lead to frustration and disappointment. By setting achievable goals, we build confidence and maintain a positive mindset. Relevant goals are aligned with our values, aspirations, and overall self-development plan. They contribute to our growth and bring us closer to becoming the best version of ourselves.

Time-bound goals have a clear deadline or timeframe. They create a sense of urgency and prevent procrastination. By setting deadlines, we hold ourselves accountable and ensure that we stay on track. Breaking down long-term goals into smaller, manageable milestones can help us stay motivated and focused throughout the process.

To create SMART goals, start by identifying what you want to achieve. Be specific about the outcome you desire and why it is important to you. Next, break down your goal into measurable steps or milestones. This will allow you to track your progress and make adjustments if necessary. Ensure that your goals are realistic and achievable, considering your current resources and capabilities.

Additionally, make sure that your goals are relevant to your self-development journey. They should align with your overall vision and values. Finally, set a deadline or timeframe for each goal. This will provide a sense of urgency and help you stay accountable.

By creating SMART goals, you can effectively navigate the path of self-development. They provide clarity, motivation, and a roadmap for personal growth. Remember, the journey towards self-development is a continuous process, and setting SMART goals will help you stay focused and empowered along the way.

Prioritizing Goals

In the journey of self-development, one of the most crucial steps is prioritizing goals. It is essential to identify and focus on the things that truly matter to us in order to achieve success and fulfillment in life. Whether you are a student, a professional, or someone looking to improve various aspects of your life, setting priorities will guide you towards your desired destination.

Setting goals is the first step towards prioritization. Take some time to reflect on what you truly want to achieve. Ask yourself questions like, "What are my long-term aspirations?" or "What do I want to accomplish in the next year?" Write down your goals, both big and small, and be specific about what you want to accomplish.

After defining your goals, it is crucial to prioritize them. Not all goals are created equal, and some may require more time, effort, or resources than others. Categorize your goals into short-term and long-term objectives. Short-term goals are those that can be achieved within a few weeks or months, while long-term goals may take years to accomplish. Prioritize your goals based on their importance, urgency, and alignment with your values.

To effectively prioritize, it is essential to consider the bigger picture. Evaluate the impact each goal will have on your overall well-being and personal growth. Some goals may contribute more significantly to your long-term happiness and satisfaction, while others may be more trivial in the grand scheme of things. By focusing on goals that align with your values and bring you closer to your ideal self, you are more likely to experience a sense of purpose and fulfillment.

Once you have identified your priorities, it is important to allocate your time and resources accordingly. Create a schedule or action plan that reflects your priorities. Break down your goals into smaller, manageable tasks and allocate specific time slots to work towards each one. By dedicating time and energy to your priorities, you will be able to make progress and achieve your desired outcomes.

Remember that priorities may change over time as circumstances evolve and new opportunities arise. Regularly review and reassess your goals to ensure they are still aligned with your values and aspirations. Be flexible and open to adapting your priorities as needed.

Prioritizing goals is a crucial skill in self-development. By setting clear goals, evaluating their importance, and allocating your time and resources accordingly, you will be on your way to mastering life's challenges and achieving the success and fulfillment you desire. Start today and take the first step towards prioritizing your goals for a brighter future.

Tracking Progress and Celebrating Milestones

In our journey of self-development, it is crucial to track our progress and celebrate the milestones we achieve along the way. This subchapter will explore the significance of monitoring our growth and how acknowledging our accomplishments can fuel our motivation.

Tracking progress allows us to have a clear understanding of where we are and how far we have come. It provides us with valuable insights into our strengths, weaknesses, and areas that require improvement. When we keep a record of our achievements, no matter how small or insignificant they may seem, we create a visual representation of our progress. This visual reminder serves as a powerful motivator, encouraging us to persevere and continue striving for further personal growth.

There are various methods to track progress, and it is important to find a system that works best for you. Some individuals prefer writing in a journal, while others may choose to use digital tools or apps. Whatever method you choose, ensure that it is something you can easily access and update regularly. By tracking our progress consistently, we can identify patterns and trends, enabling us to make more informed decisions and adjustments to our self-development strategies.

Celebrating milestones is equally important in our journey of self-development. It provides us with a sense of accomplishment and empowers us to keep pushing forward. Milestones can be both big and small, and it is crucial to acknowledge each one. Whether it is completing a challenging task, overcoming a personal fear, or reaching a specific goal, every achievement deserves recognition.

Celebrating milestones can take various forms, depending on your preferences. It can be treating yourself to something you enjoy, sharing your accomplishment with loved ones, or even taking a moment to reflect on your journey and appreciate how far you have come. The key is to find a way that resonates with you and allows you to savor the achievement.

In conclusion, tracking progress and celebrating milestones are integral aspects of self-development. By monitoring our growth, we gain valuable insights into our journey and can make informed decisions for further improvement. Celebrating milestones fuels our motivation and provides a sense of accomplishment, empowering us to keep striving for personal growth. Embrace the power of tracking progress and celebrating milestones, and let them guide you on your path to mastering life's challenges.

Chapter 4: Developing a Growth Mindset

Understanding Fixed vs. Growth Mindset

In our journey of self-development, one of the most crucial aspects to understand is the difference between a fixed mindset and a growth mindset. Both mindsets play a significant role in shaping our attitudes, beliefs, and actions towards life's challenges. By gaining a deeper understanding of these mindsets, we can unlock our potential and achieve greater success in various areas of our lives.

A fixed mindset is characterized by the belief that our qualities, abilities, and intelligence are fixed traits and cannot be changed. People with a fixed mindset often avoid challenges, shy away from taking risks, and perceive failures as a reflection of their incompetence. They tend to seek validation and avoid situations that might challenge their self-image, ultimately hindering their personal growth.

On the other hand, a growth mindset is the belief that our qualities and abilities can be developed through dedication, effort, and continuous learning. Individuals with a growth mindset embrace challenges, persist in the face of setbacks, and view failures as opportunities for growth and learning. They understand that their potential is limitless and are willing to step out of their comfort zones to pursue their goals.

Developing a growth mindset requires a shift in our thinking patterns and beliefs. It involves recognizing and challenging our fixed mindset tendencies, such as the fear of failure or the need for constant validation. By embracing a growth mindset, we open ourselves up to new possibilities and foster a positive attitude towards personal and professional development.

One powerful way to cultivate a growth mindset is through self-reflection and self-awareness. By examining our thoughts, beliefs, and reactions to challenges, we can identify areas where a fixed mindset may be holding us back. We can then consciously choose to reframe our thoughts and adopt a growth-oriented perspective.

Additionally, surrounding ourselves with individuals who embody a growth mindset can have a profound impact on our own mindset. Engaging in meaningful conversations, seeking feedback, and learning from others' experiences can inspire and motivate us to adopt a growth mindset in our own lives.

Understanding the difference between a fixed mindset and a growth mindset is essential for anyone on a journey of self-development. By embracing a growth mindset, we empower ourselves to overcome obstacles, adapt to change, and continuously evolve as individuals. Through conscious effort and a commitment to personal growth, we can master life's challenges and unlock our full potential.

Embracing Challenges and Failure

In the journey of self-development, embracing challenges and failure is an integral aspect that often gets overlooked. We live in a society that glorifies success and achievement, often disregarding the valuable lessons hidden within our struggles. However, it is through facing challenges head-on and accepting failure as a stepping stone that we can truly unlock our potential and master life's challenges.

Challenges are not meant to break us but to shape us into stronger individuals. They push us outside of our comfort zones, allowing us to discover our hidden talents and strengths. By embracing challenges, we learn to adapt, think creatively, and develop resilience. Each obstacle we encounter presents an opportunity for growth and self-improvement. It is during these moments that we truly discover who we are and what we are capable of achieving.

Failure, on the other hand, is often seen as a negative outcome. However, it is important to reframe our perspective and view failure as a stepping stone towards success. Thomas Edison once said, "I have not failed. I've just found 10,000 ways that won't work." Failure provides us with valuable feedback and teaches us valuable lessons that success cannot. It encourages us to reassess our strategies, learn from our mistakes, and try again with a renewed sense of determination. Without failure, there can be no growth or progress.

Embracing challenges and failure requires a shift in mindset. Instead of fearing them, we must approach them with curiosity and an open mind. By reframing challenges as opportunities and failure as feedback, we can transform our experiences into stepping stones towards self-development. It is through these experiences that we gain wisdom, resilience, and the ability to navigate through life's uncertainties.

To truly embrace challenges and failure, we must cultivate self-compassion. We are often our harshest critics, but it is important to remember that we are only human and bound to make mistakes. Treat yourself with kindness and understanding, and celebrate the small victories along the way. By doing so, you create a safe space to learn, grow, and embrace challenges with confidence.

In conclusion, embracing challenges and failure is an essential aspect of self-development. It is through these experiences that we discover our true potential and learn valuable life lessons. By shifting our mindset, reframing challenges and failure, and cultivating self-compassion, we can transform our lives and master life's challenges. So, embrace the challenges that come your way, learn from your failures, and watch yourself grow into the best version of yourself.

Cultivating a Positive Attitude

In the journey of self-development, one of the most crucial elements is cultivating a positive attitude. A positive attitude is not only essential for personal growth but also plays a significant role in navigating life's challenges. It is a powerful tool that can transform our outlook on life, enhance our relationships, and ultimately lead us towards success and fulfillment.

A positive attitude is about adopting an optimistic mindset and focusing on the good, even in the face of adversity. It is about choosing to see opportunities instead of obstacles, finding solutions instead of dwelling on problems, and maintaining a hopeful outlook regardless of the circumstances. When we cultivate a positive attitude, we open ourselves up to endless possibilities and create a foundation for personal growth and self-improvement.

One of the first steps in cultivating a positive attitude is to practice gratitude. Gratitude allows us to shift our perspective from what we lack to what we have. By acknowledging and appreciating the blessings in our lives, we begin to cultivate a sense of contentment and joy. Regularly expressing gratitude through journaling, meditation, or simply sharing our appreciation with others can have a profound impact on our mindset and overall well-being.

Another crucial aspect of cultivating a positive attitude is self-belief. Building self-confidence and believing in our abilities is vital for personal development. When we have faith in ourselves, we are more likely to take risks, overcome obstacles, and seize opportunities. Developing self-belief can be achieved through setting and achieving small goals, celebrating our successes, and surrounding ourselves with positive and supportive individuals.

Additionally, it is essential to practice positive self-talk. Our thoughts have a powerful influence on our emotions and actions. By replacing negative self-talk with positive affirmations, we can rewire our minds and cultivate a more optimistic attitude. Affirmations such as "I am capable," "I am deserving of happiness," and "I can handle any challenge" can empower us to face life's difficulties with resilience and determination.

Lastly, cultivating a positive attitude requires embracing a growth mindset. Recognizing that challenges and setbacks are opportunities for learning and growth allows us to approach them with a positive outlook. Instead of viewing failures as definitive, we can see them as stepping stones towards success. Embracing a growth mindset enables us to persevere, adapt, and continuously improve ourselves.

In conclusion, cultivating a positive attitude is an essential aspect of self-development. By practicing gratitude, building self-belief, embracing positive self-talk, and adopting a growth mindset, we can transform our lives and overcome any challenges that come our way. With a positive attitude, we can navigate life's ups and downs with grace, resilience, and a sense of fulfillment. So, let us embrace the power of positivity and master life's challenges together.

Nurturing Resilience and Perseverance

Resilience and perseverance are two essential qualities that can greatly contribute to self-development. In the face of life's challenges and obstacles, cultivating these traits can help us navigate through tough times and emerge stronger than ever. This subchapter aims to explore the importance of nurturing resilience and perseverance, providing practical tips and insights for individuals seeking personal growth and self-improvement.

Resilience can be defined as the ability to bounce back from difficult situations and adapt to change. It is not about avoiding hardships, but rather about developing the skills and mindset to overcome them. Resilient individuals possess a positive attitude, optimism, and a strong sense of self-belief. They view setbacks as opportunities for growth and learning, rather than as failures. By embracing resilience, we can develop the capacity to face any challenge head-on and emerge victorious.

Perseverance complements resilience by emphasizing the importance of persistence and determination. It is the ability to keep going, even when faced with obstacles and setbacks. Perseverance requires a clear vision, passion, and unwavering commitment towards achieving our goals. It pushes us to stay focused, work hard, and never give up, even when the going gets tough. Without perseverance, resilience alone may falter. However, when combined, these qualities create an unstoppable force that propels us towards personal growth and success.

So how can we nurture resilience and perseverance in our lives? Firstly, it is crucial to develop a growth mindset. Embrace challenges as opportunities for learning and growth, rather than as threats. Secondly, practice self-care and cultivate emotional well-being. Take care of your physical health, engage in activities that bring you joy, and surround yourself with positive influences. Thirdly, build a support system. Surround yourself with individuals who believe in your potential and can provide encouragement and guidance during difficult times.

Additionally, setting realistic goals and breaking them down into smaller, manageable tasks can help maintain motivation and prevent overwhelm. Celebrate each milestone achieved, no matter how small, and use these successes as fuel to keep going. Lastly, embrace failure as a stepping stone towards success. Learn from your mistakes, adapt your approach, and keep moving forward.

In conclusion, nurturing resilience and perseverance is crucial for personal growth and self-development. By cultivating these qualities, we can face life's challenges with confidence, adaptability, and unwavering determination. Remember, resilience and perseverance are skills that can be developed over time. With dedication and practice, you can master life's challenges and unlock your true potential. So, embrace resilience, cultivate perseverance, and let them guide you towards a fulfilling and successful life.

Chapter 5: Building Self-Confidence

Recognizing and Utilizing Strengths

In our journey of self-development, it is essential to understand the importance of recognizing and utilizing our strengths. Each one of us possesses unique abilities and talents that, when harnessed effectively, can propel us towards success and fulfillment. This subchapter aims to guide and inspire individuals from all walks of life on how to identify their strengths and leverage them to overcome life's challenges.

Recognizing our strengths begins with self-awareness. We must take the time to reflect on our experiences, skills, and natural inclinations. What activities do we enjoy? What tasks do we excel at? By answering these questions, we can start to uncover our core strengths. It could be anything from creativity, leadership, problem-solving, or empathy. No strength is too small or insignificant.

Once we have identified our strengths, the next step is to utilize them effectively. Understanding how to leverage our strengths can enhance our personal and professional lives. For instance, if we possess great communication skills, we can leverage them to build stronger relationships, negotiate effectively, or even pursue a career in public speaking.

One powerful way to utilize our strengths is by aligning them with our goals and aspirations. By recognizing our strengths and understanding how they contribute to our desired outcomes, we can create a roadmap to success. For example, if we have a talent for organization and planning, we can use these strengths to break down our goals into manageable tasks and create a structured action plan.

It is also important to remember that recognizing and utilizing strengths does not mean ignoring weaknesses. While it is essential to acknowledge our weaknesses, focusing too much on them can hinder our progress. Instead, we should aim to develop strategies to overcome our weaknesses or find ways to minimize their impact.

Moreover, recognizing and utilizing strengths can have a positive impact on our overall well-being. When we engage in activities that align with our strengths, we experience a sense of fulfillment, joy, and confidence. By leveraging our strengths, we can increase our self-esteem and develop a positive mindset, enabling us to face life's challenges with resilience and determination.

In conclusion, recognizing and utilizing our strengths is a fundamental aspect of self-development. By understanding our unique abilities and leveraging them effectively, we can unlock our full potential and navigate life's challenges with greater ease. So, let us take the time to identify our strengths, align them with our goals, and harness their power to create a fulfilling and successful life journey. Remember, your strengths are your superpowers – embrace them!

Overcoming Self-Doubt and Insecurity

Introduction:
Self-doubt and insecurity can be significant barriers to personal growth and self-development. They often prevent individuals from pursuing their dreams, taking risks, or even believing in their own abilities. In this subchapter, we will explore effective strategies to overcome self-doubt and insecurity, empowering you to embrace life's challenges with confidence.

Understanding Self-Doubt and Insecurity:
Self-doubt and insecurity are common feelings experienced by individuals in various aspects of life. They arise from a lack of self-belief, fear of failure, or negative past experiences. Recognizing these emotions is the first step towards conquering them.

Challenge Negative Thought Patterns:
One powerful technique for overcoming self-doubt is challenging negative thought patterns. Start by identifying the negative thoughts that fuel your insecurity and self-doubt. Ask yourself if these thoughts are based on reality or if they are distorted perceptions. Replace these negative thoughts with positive affirmations and remind yourself of your past successes.

Embrace Failure as a Learning Opportunity:
Fear of failure often contributes to self-doubt and insecurity. However, failure is an essential part of personal growth and development. Embrace failure as a learning opportunity and reframe it as a stepping stone towards success. Understand that setbacks are temporary and view them as valuable lessons that will help you improve and grow.

Cultivate   Self-Compassion:
Self-compassion is crucial in overcoming self-doubt and insecurity. Treat yourself with kindness, understanding, and forgiveness. Recognize that everyone makes mistakes and experiences self-doubt at times. Practice self-care activities, such as meditation, journaling, or pursuing hobbies that make you feel good about yourself.

Surround   Yourself   with   Supportive   Individuals:
Building a support network of like-minded individuals who uplift and encourage you is vital for overcoming self-doubt and insecurity. Surround yourself with people who believe in your abilities and provide constructive feedback. Seek out mentors or coaches who can guide you on your self-development journey.

Take   Action   and   Celebrate   Small   Wins:
Taking action is crucial in overcoming self-doubt. Start by setting small, achievable goals that align with your self-development aspirations. As you accomplish these goals, celebrate your small wins and acknowledge your progress. Doing so will boost your confidence and motivate you to continue pushing forward.

Conclusion:
Overcoming self-doubt and insecurity is a transformative journey towards self-development. By challenging negative thought patterns, embracing failure, cultivating self-compassion, surrounding yourself with supportive individuals, and taking consistent action, you can conquer self-doubt and unlock your true potential. Embrace this chapter as a guide to mastering life's challenges and achieving personal growth. Remember, you have the power to overcome self-doubt and insecurity, and the world is waiting for your unique contributions.

Practicing Self-Compassion

Self-compassion is the foundation of personal growth and development. It is the act of treating oneself with kindness, understanding, and acceptance, especially during challenging times. In the journey of self-development, it is essential to cultivate self-compassion as it enables us to navigate life's challenges with grace and resilience.

Often, we tend to be our harshest critics, setting unrealistic expectations and berating ourselves for our perceived shortcomings. However, self-compassion encourages us to embrace our imperfections and acknowledge that we are only human. It allows us to be gentle with ourselves, offering the same level of care and empathy that we would extend to a dear friend or loved one.

One aspect of practicing self-compassion involves self-acceptance. This means acknowledging our strengths and weaknesses without judgment. It involves recognizing that we are constantly evolving and that our mistakes do not define us. By accepting ourselves, flaws and all, we create a solid foundation for growth and development.

Another critical component of self-compassion is self-care. In the hustle and bustle of everyday life, it is easy to neglect our well-being. However, self-compassion emphasizes the importance of prioritizing self-care activities such as exercise, healthy eating, adequate rest, and engaging in activities that bring us joy. By taking care of ourselves, we replenish our physical, mental, and emotional energy, enabling us to face life's challenges with renewed vigor.

Self-compassion also involves practicing self-forgiveness. We all make mistakes and experience setbacks, but dwelling on them only perpetuates negativity. By forgiving ourselves for past shortcomings, we free ourselves from the burden of guilt and can focus on moving forward. It is through self-forgiveness that we can learn from our past experiences and grow into a better version of ourselves.

Lastly, self-compassion encourages us to cultivate a positive and supportive inner dialogue. Instead of engaging in self-criticism and negative self-talk, we can choose to speak to ourselves with kindness and encouragement. By nurturing a compassionate inner voice, we foster a sense of self-worth and resilience that allows us to overcome any obstacles.

In conclusion, practicing self-compassion is an integral part of self-development. By embracing self-acceptance, prioritizing self-care, practicing self-forgiveness, and nurturing a positive inner dialogue, we pave the way for personal growth, resilience, and a fulfilled life. Remember, you are worthy of compassion and kindness – embrace it, and watch yourself flourish.

Enhancing Self-Image and Body Positivity

In today's society, where beauty standards are often unattainable and unrealistic, it is crucial to prioritize enhancing self-image and promoting body positivity. This subchapter aims to guide individuals on a journey towards self-development, where they can learn to love and appreciate themselves just as they are.

Self-image is a powerful force that influences our thoughts, actions, and overall well-being. When we have a positive self-image, we feel confident, capable, and worthy. On the other hand, a negative self-image can lead to feelings of inadequacy, low self-esteem, and even mental health issues. Therefore, it is essential to cultivate a healthy self-image by focusing on self-acceptance and self-care.

To begin the journey towards enhancing self-image, it is vital to practice self-compassion. Acknowledge that nobody is perfect, and imperfections are what make us unique and beautiful. Treat yourself with kindness, forgive your mistakes, and focus on your strengths and accomplishments. Surround yourself with positive influences, whether it be supportive friends, uplifting media, or engaging in activities that make you feel good about yourself.

In addition to self-compassion, body positivity plays a significant role in our self-image. Society often dictates what is considered "beautiful," but it is crucial to challenge these narrow definitions and embrace diverse body types, sizes, and shapes. Remember that beauty comes in all forms, and what truly matters is how you feel about yourself, not how others perceive you.

To foster body positivity, engage in activities that make you feel good in your own skin. This could involve regular exercise, not to achieve a certain body shape but for the sake of feeling strong and healthy. Surround yourself with positive affirmations, whether it be through daily mantras, sticky notes with uplifting messages, or reading books that promote body positivity and self-love.

Lastly, it is important to remember that self-development is a lifelong journey. It requires ongoing effort and self-reflection. Embrace the process, celebrate small victories along the way, and be patient with yourself. Remember that you are deserving of love, happiness, and acceptance, regardless of your appearance or perceived flaws.

In conclusion, enhancing self-image and promoting body positivity are essential aspects of self-development. By practicing self-compassion, challenging societal beauty standards, and engaging in activities that make us feel good about ourselves, we can cultivate a positive self-image and embrace our bodies with love and acceptance. Remember, you are unique, beautiful, and deserving of self-love, no matter who you are or what stage of life you are in.

Chapter 6: Improving Emotional Intelligence

Understanding Emotional Intelligence

Emotional intelligence is a crucial aspect of personal growth and self-development. It encompasses the ability to recognize, understand, and manage our own emotions, as well as the emotions of others. In this subchapter, we will delve into the depths of emotional intelligence, exploring its significance and practical strategies for its enhancement.

Emotional intelligence plays a fundamental role in our relationships, work, and overall well-being. It allows us to navigate through life's challenges with grace and resilience, fostering healthier connections and better decision-making. By understanding and harnessing emotional intelligence, we can lead more fulfilling lives and achieve personal and professional success.

To comprehend emotional intelligence, we must first recognize its key components. These include self-awareness, self-regulation, empathy, motivation, and social skills. Self-awareness involves understanding our own emotions, strengths, weaknesses, and values. Self-regulation empowers us to manage our emotions effectively, avoiding impulsive or destructive behaviors. Empathy enables us to understand and relate to the feelings of others, fostering stronger connections. Motivation drives us to set and achieve meaningful goals, while social skills allow us to build and maintain healthy relationships.

Cultivating emotional intelligence requires a combination of self-reflection, self-discipline, and empathy. Developing self-awareness involves paying attention to our emotions, thoughts, and behaviors, recognizing patterns and triggers. By practicing self-regulation, we can learn to control our emotional responses and choose more constructive actions. Empathy can be fostered by actively listening to others, trying to understand their perspectives, and demonstrating compassion.

Enhancing emotional intelligence also involves developing effective communication skills, conflict resolution techniques, and stress management strategies. These skills enable us to express ourselves assertively, resolve conflicts amicably, and cope with stress in a healthy manner. Furthermore, engaging in activities such as mindfulness and journaling can help us develop a deeper understanding of our emotions and build resilience.

In conclusion, emotional intelligence is a vital aspect of self-development that impacts every facet of our lives. By nurturing our emotional intelligence, we can improve our relationships, excel in our careers, and lead more fulfilling lives. This subchapter has provided an overview of emotional intelligence and introduced practical strategies for its development. By embracing our emotions and learning to manage them effectively, we can master life's challenges and unlock our true potential. Remember, emotional intelligence is not fixed, but rather a skill that can be cultivated and refined throughout our lifetime.

Managing and Expressing Emotions

Emotions are an integral part of our human experience. They shape how we perceive and interact with the world around us. Learning to manage and express our emotions effectively is essential for our overall well-being and personal growth. In this subchapter, we will explore various strategies and techniques to help you navigate the complex world of emotions and develop a healthy emotional intelligence.

Understanding your emotions is the first step towards effective management. Emotions can range from joy and excitement to sadness and anger. By becoming aware of your emotional state, you can gain insights into your thoughts, behaviors, and patterns. Take the time to reflect on your emotions and identify the underlying causes. This self-awareness will empower you to respond more consciously and constructively.

Once you have acknowledged and understood your emotions, it is crucial to learn how to express them appropriately. Suppressing or ignoring your emotions can lead to increased stress and even physical health issues. Find healthy outlets for your emotions, such as talking to a trusted friend, writing in a journal, or engaging in creative activities like painting or dancing. Expressing your emotions in a constructive manner allows for personal growth and fosters stronger relationships with others.

Managing emotions also involves developing coping mechanisms for dealing with difficult emotions. When faced with overwhelming feelings, practice deep breathing exercises, meditation, or engage in physical activities like yoga or running. These techniques can help calm your mind and restore emotional balance. Additionally, learning to reframe negative thoughts and practicing gratitude can shift your perspective and promote a more positive emotional state.

It is important to note that managing and expressing emotions is a continuous process. It requires patience, self-compassion, and a willingness to learn and adapt. As you navigate life's challenges, remember that emotions are a natural part of being human. Embrace them, learn from them, and use them as a catalyst for personal growth.

In conclusion, mastering the art of managing and expressing emotions is a vital aspect of self-development. By understanding and acknowledging your emotions, finding healthy outlets for expression, and developing effective coping mechanisms, you can navigate life's challenges with resilience and grace. Embrace the journey of emotional growth, and you will discover a newfound sense of self-awareness, fulfillment, and connection with others.

Developing Empathy and Understanding Others

In the journey of self-development, one of the most crucial skills we can cultivate is empathy – the ability to understand and share the feelings of others. Empathy allows us to form deeper connections, build healthier relationships, and navigate life's challenges with grace and compassion. In this subchapter, we will explore the importance of developing empathy and provide practical tips to enhance this essential skill.

Empathy is not only about putting ourselves in someone else's shoes; it goes beyond sympathy or pity. It requires active listening, open-mindedness, and a genuine desire to understand others without judgment. By developing empathy, we can break down barriers, bridge differences, and foster a more inclusive and understanding world.

The first step in developing empathy is to cultivate self-awareness. Understanding our own emotions, biases, and experiences helps us relate to others on a deeper level. By acknowledging our own struggles, we become more compassionate and better equipped to support others in their own journeys.

Active listening is another fundamental aspect of empathy. It involves giving our full attention, showing genuine interest, and seeking to understand the speaker's perspective. By actively listening, we create a safe space for others to express themselves and feel heard, fostering trust and empathy in the process.

Practicing empathy also entails recognizing and respecting individual differences. Every person has unique experiences, beliefs, and values that shape their worldview. By embracing diversity and seeking to understand different perspectives, we broaden our own horizons and grow as individuals.

Another valuable tool for developing empathy is the art of asking open-ended questions. By asking thought-provoking questions, we encourage others to share their thoughts and feelings, enabling us to gain a deeper understanding of their experiences. This helps us to avoid assumptions and stereotypes, fostering genuine connections based on empathy and understanding.

Lastly, it is essential to practice empathy not only in our personal lives but also in our interactions with the world at large. By being mindful of others' perspectives, needs, and emotions, we can contribute to positive change, create harmony in our communities, and ultimately, make a difference in the lives of those around us.

In conclusion, developing empathy is a transformative skill that benefits both ourselves and others. By cultivating self-awareness, practicing active listening, embracing diversity, asking open-ended questions, and applying empathy in our daily lives, we can become more compassionate individuals and contribute to a more empathetic and understanding society. Let us embark on this journey of self-development, knowing that empathy has the power to change lives and make the world a better place for all.

Resolving Conflicts and Building Strong Relationships

In the journey of self-development, one of the most crucial skills to acquire is the ability to resolve conflicts and build strong relationships. Whether it is in our personal or professional lives, conflicts are inevitable, and how we handle them can have a significant impact on our overall well-being and success.

Conflict resolution involves finding peaceful and constructive ways to address disagreements and misunderstandings. It requires empathy, effective communication, and a willingness to understand different perspectives. By mastering conflict resolution techniques, we can transform conflicts into opportunities for growth and create stronger relationships.

First and foremost, it is essential to cultivate self-awareness. Understanding our own emotions, triggers, and biases allows us to approach conflicts with a calm and rational mindset. Taking a moment to reflect on our feelings and motivations can help us respond rather than react impulsively. This self-awareness also helps us recognize when we may be contributing to the conflict and take responsibility for our actions.

Active listening is another vital skill in resolving conflicts. By truly listening to the other person's perspective without interrupting or judging, we show respect and create a safe space for open dialogue. Paraphrasing and summarizing their points can demonstrate our understanding and validate their feelings, fostering a sense of empathy and connection.

Building strong relationships goes hand in hand with conflict resolution. It requires trust, mutual respect, and effective communication. Regularly expressing appreciation, offering support, and being open to feedback can strengthen relationships and create a foundation of trust. Additionally, being mindful of non-verbal cues, such as body language and tone of voice, can help us communicate more effectively and ensure our message is received as intended.

Moreover, it is crucial to remember that conflicts are not always negative. They can provide opportunities for growth, increased understanding, and creative problem-solving. By embracing conflicts as learning experiences, we can approach them with curiosity and a willingness to find common ground. Collaborative problem-solving techniques, such as brainstorming and compromising, can help reach win-win solutions that satisfy the needs of all parties involved.

In conclusion, mastering conflict resolution and building strong relationships is a fundamental aspect of self-development. By cultivating self-awareness, practicing active listening, and embracing conflicts as opportunities for growth, we can navigate conflicts with grace and build stronger, more fulfilling relationships. These skills not only enhance our personal lives but also contribute to our success in various professional settings. So, let us embrace conflicts as stepping stones on our path to self-development and create a world of understanding and harmony.

Chapter 7: Enhancing Communication Skills

Active Listening

In our fast-paced and increasingly digital world, it is becoming more and more difficult to truly listen and connect with others. We live in a society where everyone seems to be talking, but very few are actually listening. However, mastering the art of active listening can have profound effects on our personal and professional lives. This subchapter will delve into the importance of active listening, the benefits it brings, and practical tips to develop this invaluable skill.

Active listening is not just hearing the words someone else is saying; it involves fully engaging with the speaker and comprehending their message. By actively listening, we demonstrate respect, empathy, and interest in the person speaking. It is a skill that can enhance our relationships, deepen our understanding, and even resolve conflicts more effectively.

The benefits of active listening are numerous. Firstly, it allows us to build stronger connections with others. By truly hearing and understanding someone, we create an environment of trust and openness, fostering deeper relationships. Secondly, active listening helps us gain new perspectives and insights. By setting aside our own assumptions and judgments, we open ourselves up to learning from others' experiences and knowledge. This can lead to personal growth and self-development.

To become an active listener, we must focus on three key elements: attention, empathy, and response. Firstly, we need to give our full attention to the speaker, eliminating distractions and genuinely tuning in to their words. This means putting away our phones, turning off the TV, and maintaining eye contact. Secondly, we must practice empathy. This involves putting ourselves in the speaker's shoes and trying to understand their emotions, thoughts, and experiences. By empathizing, we create a safe space for open communication. Finally, active listening requires a thoughtful response. This can be in the form of verbal cues like summarizing or asking clarifying questions, or nonverbal cues such as nodding or smiling. These responses demonstrate that we are truly engaged in the conversation.

In conclusion, active listening is a vital skill for self-development and building meaningful relationships. By mastering this art, we can improve our communication abilities, gain new perspectives, and deepen our connections with others. So, let us make a conscious effort to become active listeners and reap the rewards it brings in all aspects of our lives.

Effective Verbal Communication

In today's fast-paced world, effective verbal communication has become an essential skill for success in every aspect of life. Whether it's in personal relationships, professional interactions, or even social settings, the ability to express oneself clearly and confidently is paramount. This subchapter aims to provide you with valuable insights and practical techniques to enhance your verbal communication skills, enabling you to navigate life's challenges with ease.

First and foremost, it is crucial to understand that effective verbal communication is a two-way process. It involves not only expressing your thoughts and ideas clearly but also actively listening to others. Listening attentively and empathetically allows you to understand the perspectives and feelings of those around you, fostering better connections and avoiding misunderstandings.

One key aspect of effective verbal communication is choosing your words carefully. Words have the power to uplift, inspire, and motivate, but they can also hurt and damage relationships if used carelessly. By being mindful of the impact your words can have on others, you can create a positive and supportive communication environment.

Another vital element of effective verbal communication is non-verbal cues. These include body language, facial expressions, tone of voice, and gestures. Research suggests that up to 93% of communication is non-verbal, so paying attention to these cues is essential. Maintaining eye contact, using open and inviting body language, and speaking with a confident and pleasant tone can significantly enhance your communication effectiveness.

Moreover, effective verbal communication involves adapting your message to suit different audiences. Understanding the needs, preferences, and communication styles of others can help you tailor your words and delivery accordingly. This flexibility allows you to connect with others on a deeper level and ensures that your message is received and understood.

Furthermore, practicing active listening and asking clarifying questions can foster effective verbal communication. By demonstrating genuine interest and engaging in meaningful conversations, you can deepen your connections with others, build trust, and gain valuable insights.

In conclusion, effective verbal communication is a vital skill for self-development in all areas of life. By focusing on clear expression, active listening, non-verbal cues, adaptability, and active engagement, you can become a more effective communicator. Mastering this skill will not only enhance your personal and professional relationships but also empower you to tackle life's challenges with confidence and grace.

Nonverbal Communication

In the journey of self-development, one aspect that often goes unnoticed but plays a vital role in our interactions is nonverbal communication. It is not just what we say that carries meaning, but also how we say it and the nonverbal cues we give off. Understanding and harnessing the power of nonverbal communication can significantly enhance our personal and professional relationships, boost our confidence, and improve our overall communication skills.

Nonverbal communication encompasses various aspects, including body language, facial expressions, gestures, eye contact, and tone of voice. These subtle cues can convey emotions, attitudes, and intentions more effectively than words alone. By being aware of and adapting our nonverbal communication, we can establish rapport, build trust, and create stronger connections with others.

Body language is a powerful tool that can reveal our true thoughts and feelings. Simple actions like maintaining an open posture, facing the person we are speaking to, and using appropriate hand gestures can make a significant difference in how we are perceived. Similarly, maintaining eye contact demonstrates attentiveness and interest, while avoiding eye contact can indicate discomfort or disinterest.

Facial expressions are another essential element of nonverbal communication. A smile can instantly brighten a conversation and create a positive atmosphere, while a furrowed brow or raised eyebrows can convey confusion or concern. By mastering our facial expressions, we can effectively convey our emotions and intentions, fostering better understanding and connection with others.

Tone of voice is often overlooked but can greatly impact the meaning of our words. Speaking in a calm and confident manner can inspire trust and respect, whereas a harsh or uncertain tone can undermine our credibility. By being mindful of our tone, we can ensure that our message aligns with our intentions and effectively communicates our desired meaning.

To truly master nonverbal communication, it is essential to practice active listening. Paying attention to the nonverbal cues of others can provide valuable insights into their thoughts and emotions. By being fully present in conversations, we can pick up on subtle cues and respond accordingly, fostering deeper connections and understanding.

In conclusion, nonverbal communication is a crucial aspect of self-development that can significantly enhance our interactions with others. By understanding and utilizing body language, facial expressions, gestures, eye contact, and tone of voice, we can establish stronger connections, build trust, and improve our overall communication skills. By practicing active listening and being mindful of our own nonverbal cues, we can become more effective communicators and navigate life's challenges with confidence and grace.

Conflict Resolution and Assertiveness

In our journey of self-development, it is inevitable that we will encounter conflicts and challenges along the way. How we handle these conflicts can greatly impact our personal growth and relationships. This subchapter aims to explore the concepts of conflict resolution and assertiveness, providing valuable insights and practical tools for everyone seeking to enhance their self-development journey.

Conflict resolution is a vital skill that allows us to peacefully navigate disagreements and find mutually beneficial solutions. It involves understanding the root causes of conflicts and finding effective ways to address them. By mastering conflict resolution, we can cultivate healthier relationships, build trust, and foster a positive environment for personal growth.

Assertiveness, on the other hand, is the ability to express our thoughts, feelings, and needs in a clear and respectful manner. It empowers us to stand up for ourselves, set boundaries, and communicate effectively. By developing assertiveness skills, we can avoid unnecessary conflicts, improve self-esteem, and enhance our interpersonal connections.

In this subchapter, we will delve into the principles and techniques of conflict resolution and assertiveness. We will explore various conflict resolution models, such as the win-win approach, where both parties collaborate to find a solution that satisfies everyone's needs. Additionally, we will discuss active listening techniques, empathy, and effective communication strategies that can promote understanding and harmony.

Furthermore, we will delve into assertiveness training, providing practical exercises and tips to help individuals develop their assertiveness skills. We will address the fear of conflict, passive-aggressive behavior, and the importance of self-awareness in asserting oneself confidently and respectfully.

By mastering conflict resolution and assertiveness, we can transform conflicts into opportunities for growth and self-discovery. We will learn to communicate our needs effectively, negotiate compromises, and build stronger relationships based on mutual respect and understanding. These skills are not only valuable in our personal lives but also in our professional endeavors, enabling us to navigate conflicts in the workplace and collaborate more efficiently.

Ultimately, this subchapter aims to equip everyone with the essential tools to handle conflicts assertively and resolve them effectively. Through the integration of conflict resolution and assertiveness into our self-development journey, we can foster personal growth, build healthier relationships, and achieve a more fulfilling and balanced life.

Chapter 8: Cultivating Healthy Habits

Importance of Self-Care

Subchapter: Importance of Self-Care

In today's fast-paced and demanding world, it is crucial to prioritize self-care. Taking care of oneself is not a luxury but a necessity for personal growth and overall well-being. In this subchapter, we will explore the significance of self-care and how it can positively impact our lives, regardless of our individual goals or aspirations.

Self-care is about intentionally setting aside time and energy to nurture our physical, mental, and emotional health. It is not selfish; rather, it is an act of self-love and self-respect. When we neglect our own needs, we become drained, stressed, and unable to perform at our best. By making self-care a priority, we can recharge, rejuvenate, and enhance our ability to face life's challenges.

One of the primary benefits of self-care is stress reduction. When we take time to relax and unwind, we allow our bodies and minds to recover from the daily pressures we face. This can be through engaging in activities we enjoy, such as reading, practicing mindfulness, taking walks in nature, or pursuing hobbies. By managing stress effectively, we improve our overall mental and physical health.

Self-care also plays a vital role in maintaining healthy relationships. When we prioritize our well-being, we become better equipped to support and care for others. By setting boundaries and managing our own needs, we can establish healthy and balanced connections with those around us.

Furthermore, self-care fosters personal growth and self-awareness. When we engage in self-reflection and introspection, we gain a deeper understanding of ourselves. This awareness allows us to identify areas for improvement and make necessary changes in our lives. By investing in our own growth, we can become better versions of ourselves and achieve our goals more effectively.

Self-care is not a one-size-fits-all concept. It varies from person to person and can encompass a broad range of activities. It is important to find what works best for us individually. Whether it is practicing yoga, engaging in creative outlets, spending quality time with loved ones, or seeking professional help when needed, self-care should be tailored to our unique needs and preferences.

In conclusion, self-care is an essential component of self-development. By prioritizing our own well-being, we can reduce stress, improve relationships, foster personal growth, and achieve a balanced and fulfilling life. Remember, self-care is not a luxury but a necessity. Embrace it, and unlock your full potential.

Establishing a Balanced Routine

In today's fast-paced world, it is easy to feel overwhelmed and out of balance. The demands of work, family, and personal life can often leave us feeling stressed and burnt out. However, establishing a balanced routine is essential for our overall well-being and personal growth. This subchapter aims to guide you in creating a routine that promotes self-development and helps you navigate life's challenges successfully.

To begin, it is crucial to understand that a balanced routine is not just about dividing your time equally among different activities. Instead, it involves prioritizing your physical, mental, and emotional needs while managing your responsibilities effectively. By doing so, you can achieve a sense of harmony and fulfillment in all areas of your life.

One of the first steps in establishing a balanced routine is setting clear goals and priorities. Take some time to reflect on what truly matters to you and what you want to achieve. This will help you stay focused and avoid wasting time on things that are not aligned with your values and objectives.

Next, create a schedule that allows for dedicated time towards self-development activities. This can include activities like reading, journaling, meditation, exercise, or pursuing a hobby. These activities not only help you grow personally but also act as a form of self-care, allowing you to recharge and rejuvenate.

Furthermore, it is important to maintain a healthy work-life balance. While it is essential to be dedicated to your career, it is equally important to make time for your personal life and relationships. Set boundaries and allocate specific times for work and relaxation to ensure that you maintain a sense of equilibrium.

Additionally, don't forget to prioritize self-care. This includes taking care of your physical health by getting enough sleep, eating nutritious meals, and exercising regularly. It also involves nurturing your mental and emotional well-being through activities such as practicing gratitude, seeking support from loved ones, and engaging in activities that bring you joy.

Lastly, be flexible and adaptable. Life is unpredictable, and plans may change. Embrace the unexpected and learn from it rather than letting it derail your progress. Adjust your routine as needed while staying committed to your self-development journey.

In conclusion, establishing a balanced routine is crucial for self-development. By setting clear goals, prioritizing self-care, and creating a schedule that allows for personal growth, you can navigate life's challenges more effectively. Remember, finding balance is an ongoing process, and it requires self-awareness, commitment, and a willingness to adapt. Take the time to invest in yourself and create a routine that promotes your overall well-being.

Nourishing Body and Mind

In the fast-paced world we live in, it's easy to neglect our most valuable assets – our body and mind. As we strive for success and overcome life's challenges, it becomes crucial to prioritize self-development and take care of ourselves holistically. This subchapter, "Nourishing Body and Mind," delves into the essential practices that can help everyone embark on a journey of self-improvement and lead a fulfilling life.

The mind-body connection is a fundamental aspect of self-development. When we nourish both our body and mind, we create a harmonious balance that enables us to thrive in all areas of life. These practices not only enhance our physical well-being but also promote mental clarity and emotional resilience.

To nourish our bodies, we must prioritize healthy eating habits and regular exercise. A balanced diet, rich in whole foods, provides us with the necessary nutrients to fuel our bodies and minds. Additionally, engaging in physical activity strengthens our bodies, releases endorphins, and reduces stress. Whether it's yoga, running, or dance, finding an exercise routine that suits our preferences and lifestyle is crucial for maintaining optimal health.

In parallel, nourishing our minds is equally important. Engaging in activities that stimulate our intellect, such as reading, learning new skills, or engaging in creative pursuits, keeps our minds sharp and curious. Regular practice of mindfulness and meditation cultivates mental clarity, reduces anxiety, and fosters inner peace. Taking time each day to relax, reflect, and disconnect from the constant noise of the world allows us to recharge and rejuvenate our minds.

Furthermore, fostering positive relationships and social connections plays a significant role in nourishing both our body and mind. Surrounding ourselves with supportive and uplifting individuals creates an environment that encourages personal growth and emotional well-being. Engaging in meaningful conversations, sharing experiences, and offering support to others not only enriches our lives but also strengthens our sense of belonging and purpose.

Remember, self-development is a lifelong journey, and nourishing our body and mind is an integral part of it. By prioritizing healthy habits, engaging in intellectual pursuits, and fostering positive relationships, we can unlock our full potential and lead a fulfilling life. So, make a commitment to yourself today – embark on the path of self-nourishment and embrace the incredible transformation that awaits you.

Managing Stress and Building Resilience

In today's fast-paced and demanding world, stress has become an inevitable part of our lives. Whether it's due to work pressures, relationship issues, financial concerns, or health problems, stress can take a toll on our mental and physical well-being. However, by learning effective strategies to manage stress and build resilience, we can navigate life's challenges more effectively and lead a more fulfilling life.

This subchapter aims to provide practical guidance on managing stress and developing resilience, regardless of your background or current circumstances. It is a comprehensive guide that can benefit anyone seeking personal growth and self-improvement.

First and foremost, it is essential to understand the nature of stress and its impact on our well-being. We explore how stress affects our mind and body, recognizing the signs and symptoms of stress overload. By gaining this understanding, we can start taking proactive steps towards managing stress effectively.

One key aspect of stress management is the ability to develop resilience. Resilience refers to our capacity to bounce back from adversity and cope with life's challenges. We delve into the concept of resilience, exploring the characteristics of resilient individuals and the strategies they employ to overcome obstacles. By cultivating resilience, we can enhance our ability to handle stress and maintain a positive outlook even in the face of adversity.

Throughout this subchapter, we provide practical techniques and exercises to help you manage stress and build resilience. These include mindfulness practices, relaxation techniques, time management strategies, and effective communication skills. We also address the importance of self-care and offer guidance on maintaining a healthy lifestyle, including exercise, nutrition, and sleep.

Additionally, we emphasize the significance of developing a support network. We discuss the benefits of seeking social support and fostering healthy relationships, as well as the role of professional help when needed.

By engaging with this subchapter, you will gain the tools and knowledge required to effectively manage stress and build resilience. You will learn how to develop a positive mindset, cultivate emotional intelligence, and overcome obstacles with grace. Ultimately, mastering stress and building resilience will empower you to lead a more balanced, fulfilling, and successful life.

No matter where you are on your self-development journey, this subchapter provides valuable insights and practical strategies that can be applied to all aspects of your life. Take the first step towards managing stress and building resilience today, and unlock your true potential for personal growth and happiness.

Chapter 9: Embracing Change and Adaptability

Understanding the Nature of Change

Change is an inevitable part of life. From the moment we are born, we are constantly evolving, adapting, and transforming. Yet, despite its omnipresence, change can often be challenging and overwhelming. In this subchapter, we will explore the nature of change and its significance in our journey of self-development.

Change is not only external but also internal. It encompasses shifts in circumstances, relationships, beliefs, and even our own identity. It can be gradual or abrupt, planned or unexpected. Whether we embrace it or resist it, change has the power to shape our lives and open doors to new opportunities.

One of the fundamental aspects to understand about change is its inevitability. Change is a natural part of the human experience, and to resist it is to deny ourselves the chance for growth and personal development. By acknowledging and accepting change, we can cultivate resilience and adaptability, enabling us to navigate life's challenges with grace and strength.

Moreover, change is a catalyst for self-discovery and transformation. It pushes us out of our comfort zones, forcing us to confront our fears and limitations. Through change, we learn more about ourselves, our values, and our true potential. It is during these periods of change that we have the opportunity to redefine our goals, dreams, and aspirations.

However, change can also be accompanied by feelings of uncertainty and fear. It disrupts our sense of stability and familiarity, causing us to question our abilities and doubt our decisions. It is important to recognize that these emotions are normal and natural. To navigate change successfully, we must cultivate a mindset of resilience, self-compassion, and optimism.

In this subchapter, we will delve into various strategies and techniques to embrace and navigate change effectively. We will explore mindfulness practices, goal-setting strategies, and self-reflection exercises to help you embrace change as an opportunity for growth and self-improvement.

No matter where you are in your journey of self-development, understanding the nature of change is essential. By embracing change rather than fearing it, you can transform challenges into stepping stones towards a more fulfilling and purposeful life.

Remember, change is not the enemy; it is the gateway to personal growth. As you embark on this journey of self-development, embrace change with an open heart and an open mind. Your willingness to adapt and evolve will unlock the limitless possibilities that lie within you.

Overcoming Resistance to Change

Change is an inevitable part of life. Whether it is a new job, a new relationship, or a new phase in life, change constantly surrounds us. However, many of us find ourselves resisting change, clinging to the familiar and comfortable. In order to truly master life's challenges and embark on a journey of self-development, it is essential to overcome this resistance to change.

Resistance to change often stems from fear of the unknown. We become comfortable with our routines and habits, even if they may not be serving us well. Stepping out of our comfort zones can be intimidating, as it requires us to confront our fears and take risks. However, it is important to remember that growth and self-development can only occur when we embrace change and step outside of our comfort zones.

One effective way to overcome resistance to change is by shifting our mindset. Instead of viewing change as something to be feared, we can choose to see it as an opportunity for growth and personal transformation. By reframing our perspective, we can begin to see change as an exciting adventure rather than a daunting challenge.

Another crucial aspect of overcoming resistance to change is self-awareness. It is important to understand the reasons behind our resistance and explore any underlying beliefs or thought patterns that may be holding us back. By probing deeper into our fears and insecurities, we can gain a better understanding of ourselves and work towards overcoming those barriers.

Additionally, building a support system can greatly assist in overcoming resistance to change. Surrounding ourselves with like-minded individuals who are also on a journey of self-development can provide encouragement, motivation, and guidance. Sharing experiences, both successes and failures, can help us realize that we are not alone in our struggles and that change is possible.

Lastly, it is important to practice self-compassion throughout the process of overcoming resistance to change. Change can be challenging, and setbacks are inevitable. By treating ourselves with kindness and understanding, we can bounce back from setbacks and continue moving forward on our path of self-development.

In conclusion, overcoming resistance to change is a crucial step in mastering life's challenges and embarking on a journey of self-development. By shifting our mindset, cultivating self-awareness, building a support system, and practicing self-compassion, we can embrace change and discover the incredible growth and transformation that it brings. Remember, change is not something to be feared, but rather an opportunity for personal growth and self-discovery.

Adapting to New Situations

In our fast-paced and ever-changing world, the ability to adapt to new situations is crucial for personal growth and self-development. Life is full of unexpected twists and turns, and how we respond to these challenges can greatly impact our overall success and happiness.

Adapting to new situations requires a mindset of flexibility and a willingness to step outside of our comfort zones. It is about embracing change and viewing it as an opportunity for growth rather than something to be feared. When we resist change, we limit our potential and hinder our progress. However, when we embrace it, we open ourselves up to new possibilities and experiences.

One of the first steps in adapting to new situations is developing self-awareness. Understanding our strengths, weaknesses, and areas for improvement allows us to identify how we can best navigate unfamiliar territory. By recognizing our patterns of behavior and thought, we can consciously choose to respond in a more productive and adaptive way.

Another important aspect of adapting to new situations is maintaining a positive mindset. Challenges and setbacks are a natural part of life, but it is our attitude towards them that determines whether we succeed or fail. By cultivating a positive outlook and reframing obstacles as opportunities for growth, we can approach new situations with a sense of optimism and resilience.

Adapting to new situations also requires a willingness to learn and acquire new skills. The ability to acquire new knowledge and adapt our skillset is essential in today's rapidly evolving world. By embracing a lifelong learning mindset, we can stay relevant and adaptable in the face of change.

Furthermore, building a strong support network can greatly enhance our ability to adapt to new situations. Surrounding ourselves with like-minded individuals who share our values and goals can provide valuable insights and support during times of change. Seeking mentorship from those who have successfully navigated similar situations can also provide guidance and inspiration.

Ultimately, adapting to new situations is a lifelong journey that requires continuous effort and self-reflection. By embracing change, maintaining a positive mindset, acquiring new skills, and building a strong support network, we can master life's challenges and unlock our full potential.

This subchapter aims to provide practical tools and strategies for individuals seeking self-development in adapting to new situations. Whether you are a young professional navigating a new career, a recent graduate adjusting to life after college, or someone simply looking to improve your ability to handle change, this chapter will equip you with the mindset and skills needed to thrive in any situation. Remember, life's challenges are opportunities for growth – embrace them, adapt, and watch yourself soar to new heights.

Thriving in Uncertain Times

In today's fast-paced and unpredictable world, it is essential to equip ourselves with the tools and mindset necessary to navigate through life's challenges. The subchapter "Thriving in Uncertain Times" from the book "Mastering Life's Challenges: A Guide to Self-Development for All" serves as a beacon of light, guiding individuals from all walks of life towards personal growth and development during times of uncertainty.

Uncertainty can arise from various sources such as career transitions, financial instability, or personal relationships. In this subchapter, we delve deep into the core principles of self-development that can help everyone adapt, evolve, and thrive amidst uncertainty.

Firstly, we explore the power of mindset. Our thoughts shape our reality, and by cultivating a growth mindset, we can view uncertainty as an opportunity for growth rather than a hinderance. This subchapter provides practical techniques to shift our perspective, embrace change, and reframe challenges as stepping stones towards personal and professional success.

Next, we delve into the importance of self-awareness. Understanding our strengths, weaknesses, and values enables us to make informed decisions during uncertain times. Through introspection exercises and self-reflection, readers can gain a deeper understanding of themselves and their aspirations, paving the way for a more fulfilling and authentic life.

Additionally, the subchapter emphasizes the significance of resilience in uncertain times. Building resilience is like strengthening a muscle; it requires practice and perseverance. By incorporating resilience-building strategies, such as developing a support network, practicing self-care, and setting realistic goals, individuals can bounce back from setbacks and adapt to changing circumstances with grace and determination.

Furthermore, we explore the role of adaptability and flexibility. In uncertain times, the ability to adapt to new situations and embrace change becomes paramount. This subchapter provides practical tips and techniques to enhance adaptability skills, enabling readers to navigate through transitions and unexpected challenges with ease and confidence.

Lastly, the subchapter emphasizes the importance of lifelong learning. In times of uncertainty, staying curious and continuously seeking knowledge is essential. By adopting a growth mindset and cultivating a thirst for knowledge, individuals can remain agile and adaptable, staying one step ahead in an ever-changing world.

"Thriving in Uncertain Times" is a subchapter designed to empower individuals from all backgrounds with the necessary tools to not only survive but thrive in the face of uncertainty. By embracing change, cultivating resilience, and continuously developing oneself, individuals can overcome life's challenges and emerge stronger, more fulfilled, and ready to seize new opportunities. This subchapter is a valuable resource for anyone seeking personal growth and development in the realm of self-development, providing a roadmap towards mastering life's uncertainties.

Chapter 10: Sustaining Self-Development

Lifelong Learning and Growth

In the fast-paced and ever-changing world we live in, the importance of lifelong learning and personal growth cannot be overstated. Whether you are a young professional looking to climb the corporate ladder, a stay-at-home parent seeking personal fulfillment, or a retiree wanting to make the most out of your golden years, continuous self-development is the key to unlocking your true potential.

This subchapter delves into the transformative power of lifelong learning and growth, and how it can positively impact every aspect of your life. Regardless of your age, background, or current circumstances, you have the ability to embark on a journey of self-improvement that can lead to a more fulfilling and successful existence.

By engaging in lifelong learning, you open yourself up to new possibilities and opportunities. Learning doesn't have to be restricted to formal education – it can be as simple as reading books, attending workshops, or participating in online courses. The act of learning keeps your mind sharp, encourages creativity, and expands your knowledge base. It also enables you to adapt to new technologies and trends, ensuring you remain relevant in a rapidly evolving world.

Moreover, personal growth goes hand-in-hand with lifelong learning. As you acquire new knowledge and skills, you gain the confidence to step out of your comfort zone and embrace new challenges. This growth mindset allows you to overcome obstacles, learn from failures, and develop resilience. It also fosters a sense of curiosity, leading to continuous self-discovery and personal fulfillment.

In the realm of self-development, lifelong learning and growth are essential. They enable you to identify and harness your strengths, work on your weaknesses, and cultivate a growth mindset that propels you toward your goals. By investing time and effort in your personal development, you become a more well-rounded individual, capable of achieving success in all areas of your life – be it relationships, career, health, or personal happiness.

In conclusion, lifelong learning and growth are fundamental to self-development. They empower you to adapt, evolve, and thrive in an ever-changing world. Regardless of your circumstances, embrace the mindset of a lifelong learner, and commit to your personal growth journey. The rewards will be immense – a more fulfilling life, increased opportunities, and the ability to overcome any challenge that comes your way. So, embark on this transformative path today, and watch as your life unfolds into a masterpiece of self-development.

Building a Supportive Network

In the journey of self-development, one of the most crucial aspects is building a supportive network. No one can succeed in isolation, and surrounding ourselves with like-minded individuals who uplift and encourage us is essential for personal growth. This subchapter aims to guide everyone, regardless of their background or goals, on how to establish and nurture a network that supports their self-development journey.

First and foremost, it is important to recognize the power of positive relationships. Surrounding ourselves with people who share similar aspirations and values can greatly impact our mindset and motivation. Seek out individuals who inspire you, challenge you, and genuinely care about your well-being. These individuals will become your support system, offering guidance, advice, and a listening ear when needed.

However, building a supportive network goes beyond just finding like-minded individuals. It also involves cultivating relationships with people from diverse backgrounds and perspectives. By doing so, we open ourselves up to new ideas, experiences, and opportunities for personal growth. Embrace diversity within your network and be open to learning from others who may have different life experiences and knowledge.

Networking events, workshops, and conferences are excellent platforms to meet individuals who share similar interests and goals. Attend these events with an open mind and a willingness to connect with others. Engage in meaningful conversations, actively listen, and be genuinely interested in getting to know others. Remember, networking is a two-way street, so be prepared to offer support and assistance to others as well.

In addition to in-person connections, the digital world offers countless opportunities for building a supportive network. Social media platforms, online forums, and communities centered around self-development can provide a virtual space for connecting with individuals who share similar passions. Engage in these online communities, contribute valuable insights, and build meaningful connections that extend beyond the digital realm.

Lastly, it is crucial to maintain and nurture the relationships within your network. Regular communication, whether through phone calls, meetups, or virtual hangouts, is essential for staying connected. Show genuine interest in the lives and endeavors of those within your network, and be available to provide support and encouragement whenever needed. By actively investing in your relationships, you create a strong foundation of trust and support that will benefit your self-development journey for years to come.

In conclusion, building a supportive network is a vital component of self-development. Surround yourself with individuals who inspire, challenge, and uplift you. Embrace diversity within your network and be open to learning from others. Attend networking events, engage in online communities, and actively maintain your relationships. Remember, a strong support system can make all the difference in mastering life's challenges and achieving personal growth.

Continuously Evaluating and Adjusting Goals

In the journey of self-development, setting and achieving goals is a fundamental aspect. However, it is important to recognize that goals are not set in stone. They need to be regularly evaluated and adjusted to ensure they remain relevant and aligned with our evolving aspirations and circumstances. This subchapter explores the significance of continuously evaluating and adjusting goals, providing valuable insights and strategies for mastering life's challenges.

Life is an ever-changing tapestry of experiences, and as we navigate through its twists and turns, our priorities may shift, new opportunities may arise, or unforeseen obstacles may present themselves. By regularly evaluating our goals, we empower ourselves to adapt and grow in response to these changes, rather than being confined by outdated aspirations.

The process of evaluating goals involves introspection and self-reflection. It requires us to ask ourselves important questions: Are these goals still meaningful to me? Do they align with my values and passions? Are they helping me progress towards my ultimate vision of self-fulfillment? By honestly assessing the answers, we can identify which goals need adjusting or even replacing.

Adjusting goals is not a sign of failure but rather a testament to our growth and adaptability. It allows us to refine our direction, realign our efforts, and set new targets that resonate with our present circumstances. This flexibility is crucial in the pursuit of self-development, as it enables us to seize new opportunities and overcome unexpected challenges.

To effectively adjust goals, it is essential to cultivate self-awareness and maintain a growth mindset. Continuously evaluating our progress and learning from our experiences provides valuable insights that inform our decision-making. We can then adjust our goals in a way that stretches us just enough to foster growth, without overwhelming or discouraging ourselves.

In this subchapter, we will explore practical techniques for evaluating and adjusting goals. We will delve into the art of setting realistic timelines, breaking big goals into smaller, manageable steps, and leveraging feedback loops to monitor progress. Additionally, we will discuss the importance of seeking support and guidance from mentors, accountability partners, or self-development communities to ensure we stay on track and maintain focus.

Continuously evaluating and adjusting goals is not a one-time task but an ongoing practice in the pursuit of self-development. By embracing this iterative process, we empower ourselves to lead fulfilling lives, navigate challenges with resilience, and seize opportunities for growth and self-actualization. So, join us on this transformative journey and unlock your full potential.

Celebrating Personal Growth

Title: Celebrating Personal Growth

Introduction:
In this subchapter, "Celebrating Personal Growth," we delve into the profound journey of self-development and the importance of acknowledging and honoring our progress along the way. Regardless of our unique backgrounds, aspirations, or circumstances, personal growth is a universal desire that resonates with everyone. This chapter aims to inspire and empower individuals on their journey of self-discovery, providing valuable insights and practical advice to celebrate personal growth.

Embracing   Change:
Personal growth begins with a willingness to embrace change. It requires stepping out of our comfort zones, challenging limiting beliefs, and exploring new perspectives. By recognizing that change is an essential part of personal development, we can approach it with curiosity and an open mind. Celebrating personal growth means honoring the courage it takes to embark on this transformative journey.

Setting   Meaningful   Goals:
Goal setting plays a pivotal role in self-development. By defining clear and meaningful objectives, we can align our actions with our aspirations and experience a sense of purpose. Celebrating personal growth involves acknowledging the progress made towards our goals, both big and small. It is a reminder that every step taken is a step closer to becoming the best version of ourselves.

Cultivating   Resilience:

As we navigate the challenges of life, resilience becomes a vital trait for personal growth. Celebrating personal growth involves recognizing our ability to bounce back from setbacks, learn from failures, and adapt to new situations. By cultivating resilience, we can view obstacles as opportunities for growth and celebrate the strength we gain from overcoming them.

Practicing   Self-Reflection:

Self-reflection is a powerful tool for personal growth. Taking time to introspect and evaluate our thoughts, emotions, and actions allows us to gain self-awareness and make conscious choices. Celebrating personal growth means honoring the moments of self-reflection that lead to profound insights and personal breakthroughs.

Expressing   Gratitude:

Gratitude is a transformative practice that amplifies personal growth. By acknowledging and appreciating the people, experiences, and lessons that contribute to our development, we create space for more growth to occur. Celebrating personal growth involves expressing gratitude for the journey and the individuals who have supported and inspired us along the way.

Conclusion:

In the subchapter, "Celebrating Personal Growth," we explored the essential elements of self-development and the significance of honoring our progress. Whether you are just starting your journey or have been on the path of self-development for some time, remember to celebrate every milestone, big or small. Embrace change, set meaningful goals, cultivate resilience, practice self-reflection, and express gratitude. By doing so, you will unlock your full potential and experience the joy of personal growth.

Conclusion: The Journey of Self-Development

Congratulations! You have reached the end of this transformative journey towards self-development. Throughout this book, "Mastering Life's Challenges: A Guide to Self-Development for All," we have explored various aspects of personal growth and provided you with valuable tools and insights to help you navigate life's challenges.

Self-development is a lifelong journey, and this book aimed to equip you with the necessary knowledge and skills to embark on this path. We have delved into understanding oneself, setting goals, cultivating positive habits, fostering healthy relationships, managing emotions, and overcoming obstacles. By embracing these principles, you have taken the first step towards unlocking your full potential.

The journey of self-development is not a linear one. It is filled with ups and downs, twists and turns. There will be times when you feel like you have strayed from the path, but remember that setbacks are an integral part of growth. Each challenge you face is an opportunity for learning and self-discovery. Embrace them with resilience and determination, for they will shape you into a stronger and wiser individual.

As you continue on your journey, it is essential to cultivate self-compassion. Celebrate your successes, no matter how small, and acknowledge your efforts. Remember that self-development is not a race or a competition. It is about becoming the best version of yourself, at your own pace.

Surround yourself with a supportive network of like-minded individuals who share your passion for self-improvement. Seek out mentors and role models who can guide you and inspire you along the way. Share your experiences and insights with others, for by doing so, you contribute to their growth as well.

Always remember that self-development is not solely about personal gain. It is about becoming a better human being and making a positive impact on the world around you. As you continue to develop your skills and knowledge, find ways to use them for the greater good. Whether it is through volunteering, mentoring, or simply being kind and compassionate towards others, your journey of self-development can have a ripple effect that extends far beyond yourself.

In conclusion, self-development is a lifelong journey that requires dedication, self-reflection, and continuous learning. The path may not always be smooth, but with the right mindset and tools, you have the power to overcome any challenge that comes your way. Embrace the process, celebrate your growth, and remember that the journey of self-development is a truly transformative and rewarding one. May you continue to thrive and inspire others on this incredible journey of personal growth.

Milton Keynes UK
Ingram Content Group UK Ltd.
UKHW020930231123
433129UK00016B/857